THE KINGS AND QUEENS
OF SCOTLAND

THE KINGS
AND QUEENS
OF SCOTLAND

Text by
Nicholas Best

Portraits courtesy
of the National Galleries of Scotland

WEIDENFELD & NICOLSON
LONDON

First published in Great Britain in 1999
by Weidenfeld & Nicolson

A CIP catalogue record for this book is available
from the British Library
ISBN 0 297 82489 9

All photographs copyright © National Galleries of
Scotland, 1999
excluding p.24, 44, © The Trustees of the National
Museums of Scotland, 1999
and p. 88 © Mr R Hutchison (displayed in the Scottish
National Portrait Gallery)
Designed and Typeset by: Nigel Soper
Set in: Bembo

Weidenfeld & Nicolson
The Orion Publishing Group Ltd
5 Upper Saint Martin's Lane
London WC2H 9EA

FRONTISPIECE: *Charles III by Antonio David*

CONTENTS

DUNCAN I

reigned 1034–1040

Born in 1001, Duncan probably became King of Strathclyde in 1018. He inherited the rest of Scotland (except for the far north) on the death of his grandfather in 1034, and was thus the first monarch to rule over the bulk of the country as we know it today.

Duncan has achieved lasting fame as the wise and gentle ruler of Shakespeare's play *Macbeth*, brutally murdered by his cousin at the behest of Lady Macbeth. In reality, though, he was not a particularly distinguished king. He led an unsuccessful expedition against the English in Durham and was later defeated by Macbeth's forces at Cawdor in 1040 – he was either killed in the battle or murdered immediately afterwards. His sons Malcolm and Donald Bane fled the country, leaving Macbeth to rule unchallenged for the next seventeen years.

Duncan I by Isaac Taylor

MACBETH

reigned 1040–1057

Macbeth has suffered badly at the hands of William Shakespeare. Far from being the villain portrayed in Shakespeare's play, he was in fact an able man with an excellent claim to the throne. His wife was of royal descent and her brother had been murdered to prevent him claiming the throne from Duncan. Macbeth, too, was probably of royal descent.

Born in about 1005, he was mormaer (high steward) of Moray before he defeated Duncan in 1040. He ruled Scotland for the next seventeen years and was sufficiently sure of himself by 1050 to leave the country for several months to make a pilgrimage to Rome. Eventually, however, Macbeth was challenged by Duncan's son Malcolm and killed at the battle of Lumphanan in 1057 – an episode not nearly as dramatic as it is portrayed in Shakespeare's play.

Macbeth by John Hall

MALCOLM III

reigned 1058–1093

In theory, Macbeth was succeeded as king by his simple-minded stepson Lulach. In practice, Lulach was quickly murdered and Macbeth's conqueror, Malcolm, took the throne. He ruled Scotland during the Norman invasion of England and did his best to prevent the invasion spreading north of the border.

Born around 1031, he grew up in exile, only returning to Scotland as a young man. He clashed several times with William the Conqueror and his successors, not least because Malcolm's brother-in-law, Edgar, was the Saxon pretender to the English throne. It was during a Scottish invasion of Northumberland in 1093 that Malcolm was ambushed and killed by an English knight near Alnwick Castle (the site is still marked by a cross today). Malcolm and his wife Margaret – later St Margaret – were the first royal couple to live in Edinburgh Castle.

Malcolm III by Alexander Bannerman

DONALD III

reigned 1093–1097

EDMUND *reigned jointly with Donald III 1094–1097*

Donald Bane was Malcolm III's younger brother, born in about 1033. As soon as he heard of Malcolm's death he seized Edinburgh Castle with the aid of Celtic clansmen and expelled Malcolm's sons, who fled south. The move was initially very popular, because the Scottish court under Malcolm had become too English for many Scots' liking. But Malcolm's sons regrouped under Duncan, the eldest son by his first marriage.

Donald Bane was temporarily deposed in 1094, although he then formed an alliance with another of Malcolm's sons, Edmund, whereby Donald ruled Scotland north of the Clyde and Edmund ruled the south. In 1097, however, Donald Bane was deposed for the last time by another son, Edgar. As an additional precaution, he was blinded in both eyes and imprisoned for the rest of his life. He died about 1100. Edmund was spared this fate. Instead he was exiled to a monastery and died full of remorse around 1100. He was buried in chains at his own request.

Donald III by Miller

DUNCAN II

reigned 1094

As the eldest son of Malcolm III, Duncan (born about 1060) was sent to England in 1072 as a hostage for the good behaviour of his father. He was very lucky not to have been executed by William the Conqueror in reprisal for his father's invasion of northern England in 1079. Instead, William contented himself with building a new castle on the Tyne and continuing to hold Duncan prisoner.

Duncan did not get back to Scotland until 1094, when he overthrew his uncle, Donald Bane, with the aid of an English and French army. By then, however, he had become much more English than Scottish, which did not commend him to the Celtic chieftains. He was killed some time in 1094 by the mormaer (high steward) of Mearns, one of Scotland's most unruly provinces. The oldest surviving Scottish royal charter dates from his brief reign.

Duncan II by Miller

EDGAR

❖

reigned 1097–1107

Although he seized the crown by force and had his uncle blinded, Edgar (born about 1074) was actually a kind and gentle man, devoted to peace rather than to war. He never married and was very close to his mother, St Margaret. From her he inherited a pleasant, saintly temperament and an understanding of the wider world outside Scotland.

Edgar was in fact the first king to have Saxon as well as Scottish blood. His sister married Henry I of England, thus strengthening the links between the two countries. Edgar maintained good relations with the English, while discouraging their influence in Scottish affairs. He ceded the Western Isles to Norway rather than fight a bloody war, and showered the Irish king with gifts, including a camel. Edgar died in 1107, leaving a peaceful inheritance to be divided between his younger brothers Alexander and David.

Edgar by Alexander Bannerman

ALEXANDER I

✠

reigned 1107–1124

In the words of a medieval chronicler, Alexander was 'a lettered and godly man, very humble and amiable towards the clerics and regulars, but terrible beyond measure to the rest of his subjects'. He ruthlessly crushed a rebellion in Moray during his reign, yet took a keen interest in Church affairs and did much to improve the government of the country.

Born about 1077, Alexander spent his early manhood exiled in England and always remained close to the English king, Henry I, whose daughter he married. But he was also fiercely protective of Scottish interests, insisting, for instance, that the Scottish Church owed no allegiance to York or Canterbury but was accountable only to the Pope. He died peacefully in 1124, after which his brother David reunited the two halves of the country and succeeded him as King of all Scotland.

Alexander I (detail) from Scottish National Portrait Gallery
Processional Frieze by William Hole

DAVID I

※

reigned 1124–1153

One of Scotland's finest kings, David was born in 1084 and grew up with a strong sense of duty towards his subjects. He was religious and fair-minded, a keen gardener and an energetic modernizer of the state. The reforms he imposed on Scotland did much to prevent the country from being absorbed by England in later centuries.

Through his marriage to an English noblewoman, David was also a powerful force in England, with large estates in the Midlands and a claim to lands in Northumbria. After Henry I's death, David took advantage of English unrest to push Scotland's borders southwards, the furthest south they would ever go. As both man and king, he was greatly respected by everyone who knew him. It is arguable that Scotland was never again as highly regarded as it was during his reign.

David I by Alexander Bannerman

MALCOLM IV

✦

reigned 1153–1165

Born in 1142, Malcolm was only eleven when he succeeded his grandfather David. This inevitably led to unrest, particularly among the Celtic chieftains, who resented the Anglo-Normans at the Scottish court. Malcolm had to deal with several serious revolts during his reign and he did so with Norman help, which enraged the Celts still further.

Fortunately, he had inherited his grandfather's diplomatic skill and made a lasting peace with his enemies. He returned land to the English, rather than fight a losing war, and later accompanied Henry II to the siege of Toulouse. At home he supported the Church and busied himself with good government. He was nicknamed 'the Maiden' after taking a vow of celibacy, but appears to have fathered an illegitimate child at the behest of his mother, who worried about him. Malcolm died at the age of twenty-three, before he had the chance to fulfil his considerable potential.

Malcolm IV – Silver Sterling

WILLIAM I

⁜

reigned 1165–1214

Born in 1143, William succeeded his brother
Malcolm at the age of twenty-two and held
the throne against all comers for the next
forty-nine years. Physically robust, he was
known as 'the Lion', probably because of the lion
rampant on his coat of arms.

William strengthened the government of his
predecessors and was the first king to bring the north
of Scotland fully under control. He built a string of
castles in Galloway and subdued his enemies by
blinding and castrating their sons. He also founded a
number of royal burghs to consolidate his hold on the
country. Abroad he was less successful. He tried to get
Northumberland back from the English, but succeeded
only in being humiliated by Henry II. It was more by
luck than good judgement that Scotland did not
become subservient to England during his reign.

William I (detail) from Scottish National Portrait Gallery
Processional Frieze by William Hole

ALEXANDER II

reigned 1214–1249

William's son, Alexander (born in 1198), was known as 'the Peaceful', a nickname he did not entirely deserve. He chopped the hands and feet off rebels or had them torn apart by horses. The heads of his enemies were delivered to him at court and he eliminated a rival claimant to the throne, an infant girl, by having her brains dashed out against the market cross in Forfar.

He was a competent ruler nevertheless, who codified the country's laws and enforced them in all corners of the realm. His first wife was the daughter of England's King John, but this did not prevent Alexander from siding with the English barons against the king. He believed in the rule of law and was present at the signing of Magna Carta in 1215. The borders he agreed with England are still in force today.

Alexander II (detail) from Scottish National Portrait Gallery
Processional Frieze by William Hole

ALEXANDER III

reigned 1249–1286

Alexander was only eight when he succeeded his father. Two years later he married Henry III's daughter, doing homage to the English king for his English lands, but not his Scottish ones. Even aged ten, he knew better than to give anything away to the English if he could avoid it.

In 1262, Alexander launched a bid to recover the Western Isles from the King of Norway. He succeeded after a bitter struggle, and later married his daughter to the king's son. Alexander's wife and other children were all dead by 1284, so he remarried the following year in order to produce a male heir. On a stormy evening in March 1286, he left Edinburgh Castle to spend the night with his new young bride in Dunfermline, across the Forth, but his horse slipped and fell in the darkness. Alexander's body was not discovered until the next day.

'Alexander III of Scotland Rescued from the Fury of a Stag by the Intrepidity of Colin Fitzgerald' (detail) by Benjamin West

MARGARET

reigned 1286–1290

Alexander's sudden death left the succession wide open. His widow thought she was pregnant but produced no heir. His only surviving descendant therefore was his granddaughter Margaret, born in 1283 to Alexander's daughter and the new King of Norway.

But Margaret, Maid of Norway, was a child of three and had never set foot in Scotland. A group of six Guardians took control of the country until she was old enough to rule. Opposition divided into several factions, notably the Bruces and the Balliols, both of whom claimed descent from King David. The Guardians appealed to Edward I of England to help keep the peace. The issue was still unresolved when Margaret set sail from Norway in September 1290. Unfortunately, she died *en route* without ever reaching Scotland, and the house of Dunkeld died with her.

Margaret (detail) from Scottish National Portrait Gallery
Processional Frieze by William Hole

JOHN

reigned 1292–1296

No less than thirteen 'competitors' claimed the throne after Margaret's death. Rather than seize it by force, they agreed to settle the issue in court. Thus it was that a descendant of David I, John Balliol (born around 1250), became king in 1292.

But there was a heavy price to pay. In return for England's peacekeeping role in the interregnum, John was forced to accept Edward I as his overlord, something previous Scottish kings had always refused to do. With little support from his 'competitors', John was powerless to prevent Edward throwing his weight around. After a futile military campaign, he surrendered to the English in 1296 and was publicly stripped of his crown and sceptre, sword and ring. He was held prisoner until 1299, then exiled to his French estates, dying blind and forgotten in 1313.

John Balliol by J. Taylor

INTERREGNUM

⁜

1296–1306

After John Balliol's forcible removal, Scotland was without a monarch for ten years. Edward I rampaged almost at will, earning the epithet 'Hammer of the Scots'. It seemed only a matter of time before he reduced Scotland to the status of an English province, as he had already done with Wales.

But he reckoned without the fierce nationalism of the Scots. A champion arose in Sir William Wallace, who trounced the English at Stirling Bridge in 1297. He flayed the skin of an English tax collector and wore it as a belt. In reply, Edward raised another army and led it himself, defeating the Scots at Falkirk in 1298. Wallace was later hanged and disembowelled in London, his body quartered and displayed in four different towns – an episode that served only to unite the Scots in their loathing of the English.

William Wallace (detail) by W. & A. K. Johnston after David Allan

ROBERT I

reigned 1306–1329

Born in 1274, Robert the Bruce was a descendant of David I. In the chaos following John Balliol's removal, he changed sides five times, sometimes supporting Sir William Wallace, sometimes the English king. He was so disheartened by the experience that it was only the sight of a spider spinning its web, according to legend, that prompted him to keep trying and not to give up hope.

With no other obvious candidate for the throne, Robert was declared king in 1306. Luckily for him, Edward I of England died in 1307, to be succeeded by the weaker Edward II. Robert rallied the Scots against the English, crushing them at Bannockburn in 1314 and forcing them to recognize Scotland as an independent state. He arranged for his heart to be cut out after his death and taken on a crusade. Robert died of leprosy in 1329.

Robert the Bruce [or Robert I] (detail) by George Jamesone
Private Scottish Collection

DAVID II

reigned 1329–1371

It was David's bad luck to succeed an outstanding
father at the age of only five. He inherited many
of Robert the Bruce's qualities, but was pitted
against a formidable English king in Edward III,
who was as strong as Edward II had been weak. David
did well simply to hold on to his throne against fierce
opposition both at home and abroad.

His enemies were led by Edward Balliol, son of the
deposed King John, who asserted his own right to the
crown. David had to flee to France in 1334 and did not
return until 1341. He was captured by the English in
1346 and only released in 1357. Unlike Balliol, David
always refused homage to the English king, clinging
resolutely to Scottish independence even after one-
third of the population had been wiped out by the
Black Death. David died childless in 1371.

David II by Edward Harding after George Jamesone

ROBERT II

reigned 1371–1390

Davidwas succeeded by his nephew, a grandson of Robert the Bruce. Robert II was almost fifty-five when he inherited the throne – eight years older than his uncle had been. He had been popular in his youth, but was well past his prime by the time he became king.

His father was Walter Stewart, the sixth in a hereditary line of Royal Stewards – originally Anglo-Norman – who had served the Scottish monarchy for generations. Walter's marriage to Robert the Bruce's daughter had not endeared him to Scotland's barons, who found it hard to take the Stewarts seriously as kings. After thirteen years of ineffective rule, Robert II admitted defeat and handed the government over to his son, John. But a kick from a horse left John permanently disabled, almost as useless as his father. The omens did not look good when Robert died in 1390.

Robert II by James Roberts

ROBERT III

✦

reigned 1390–1406

Born in 1337, John changed his name to Robert on succeeding his father. To call himself John II would have meant acknowledging the legitimacy of John Balliol as John I. And the Balliols were still around, still claiming the throne…

Unfortunately, Robert had already been declared unfit to rule before he became king. The job was undertaken by his brother, the official Governor of the Realm. But the country slowly descended into anarchy, with no central cohesion and a growing division between the clan-based Highlanders and the more sophisticated, feudal Lowlanders. Robert felt so bad about the situation that he asked to be buried in a dung heap with the epitaph 'Here lies the worst of kings and most miserable of men'. He died in 1406, a few days after learning that his only surviving son, James, had been captured by pirates and sold to the English.

Robert III – Silver Groat

JAMES I

reigned 1406–1437

Held prisoner as a child, James (born in 1394) spent the first eighteen years of his reign in England and did not return to Scotland until 1424. In his absence, the country was governed first by his uncle, then by his cousin – both Dukes of Albany.

James was a very able man, strong, energetic and highly educated. He had accompanied Henry V to the French wars and had learned kingship from a master. His first act on returning to Scotland was to break the power of the nobles by executing their leaders, including Albany. He also humiliated the Highland chiefs by summoning them to a meeting and arresting the lot – an act of treachery that won him few friends. In 1437 he was stabbed to death in an attempted coup. But no coup took place and the assassins were themselves killed after being horribly tortured.

James I (detail) by an unknown artist

IACOBVS I D·GRATIA
REX· SCOTORVM

IACOBVS 2 D·GRA
REX·SCOTORVM

JAMES II

❖

Badly disfigured by a birthmark, 'James of the Fiery Face' was not quite seven when his father was murdered. He spent the rest of his childhood as a pawn in other people's power struggles. At the age of nine he had to be smuggled out of Edinburgh Castle in a trunk to avoid capture. A year later, he hosted a dinner at which the teenage Earl of Douglas and his brother were taken outside and beheaded.

James took control of the government in 1449 and spent much of his reign fighting to contain the power of the Douglas family. In a repeat of his childhood experience, he granted the eighth Earl a safe passage to Stirling Castle in 1452, then killed him at dinner – a betrayal that horrified the nation. He himself was killed by an exploding cannon in 1460.

James II (detail) by an unknown artist

JAMES III

⁂

reigned 1460–1488

James was only eight when he succeeded his father. He grew up cultured and artistic, with little taste for manly pursuits. There were rumours that he was homosexual, although he is known to have had a girlfriend named Daisy.

James had little interest in kingship or matters of state, preferring to spend time with his artistic friends. He was lenient and indecisive, incapable of learning from his mistakes. The inevitable rebellion against his rule was led by his own family, more in sorrow than in anger. James's favourites were hanged and he himself was held prisoner for a while. In the civil war that followed, James's forces were defeated at Sauchieburn. Fleeing from the battlefield, James fell from his horse and was taken to a mill, where he was stabbed through the heart by an unknown assassin posing as a priest. Few people mourned him.

James III (detail) by an unknown artist

ACORVS · 3 D GRATIA
REX · SOTORVM

ACOBVS · 4 · D · GRATIA
REX · SCOTORVM

JAMES IV

reigned 1488–1513

Unlike his father, James (born in 1473) was a man's man – strong, able, energetic, full of enthusiasm and ideas. He travelled constantly and inspired people wherever he went: barons, peasants, Highland chiefs and women (especially women!). His was the grandest and most glamorous court Scotland had ever seen.

James wore a heavy iron chain around his waist as penance for his youthful opposition to his father. He backed Perkin Warbeck in his bid to seize the English throne from Henry VII, but later married Henry's daughter, Margaret. He built up the Scottish navy, supported universities and a college of surgeons, and backed Scotland's first printing press. But his impetuosity got the better of him when he invaded England in 1513, an act of treachery for which he was excommunicated by the Pope. Killed at Flodden, James was denied a Christian burial.

James IV (detail) by an unknown artist

JAMES V

❖

reigned 1513–1542

As so often in Scottish history, James was just a child – seventeen months old – when he inherited the throne. At first he was left with his mother, an English Tudor, sister of Henry VIII. But she was widely distrusted by the Scots, so James was often kept away from her as he grew up.

He received little formal education after the age of twelve, which put him at a disadvantage compared with other monarchs. He was disliked by the Scottish nobility, who thought him greedy and vindictive, but was more popular with peasants, who appreciated the smack of firm government. James often moved among them disguised as a farmer, listening to their opinions and seducing their daughters. His own sons both died in 1541, leaving him distraught. James followed them a year later, after failing to rally the nation for a war against the English. He was Scotland's last Catholic king.

James V (detail) by an unknown artist

MARY

reigned 1542–1567

Half-French, Mary was less than a week old when her father died. She spent most of her childhood in France, marrying the heir to the French throne at fifteen. A year later he declared himself King of Scotland, a move that effectively ended the Auld Alliance. Fortunately he died soon afterwards, leaving Catholic Mary to return alone to Scotland in 1561.

All would have been well if she had ruled wisely, taking the advice she was given. Instead she surrounded herself with favourites, plotting to seize the English throne from her cousin Elizabeth. Pregnant by her second husband, Lord Darnley, she was present when he stabbed her companion Rizzio to death. Darnley himself was then murdered, to be succeeded as Mary's next husband by the unsuitable Lord Bothwell. The exasperated Scots forced Mary to abdicate. She fled to England, but was executed in 1587.

Mary Queen of Scots (detail) by an unknown artist after François Clouet
OVERLEAF: *'Mary Queen of Scots' Farewell to France'*
(detail) by Robert Herdman

JAMES VI/I

reigned 1567–1625

James was born in 1566, three months after the murder of his mother's companion, Rizzio, by his jealous father, Lord Darnley. Mary was forced to abdicate when James was only one. He never saw her again.

Intelligent, educated and bookish, James took control of his kingdom at the age of sixteen, in the firm belief that monarchs had a divine right to rule. In 1603 his mother's cousin, Elizabeth, died childless and James moved down to London to become James I of England. Despite being the first king to reign over both countries he returned to Scotland only once during the rest of his life. James took a shine to the English, doing his best to promote a union of his two kingdoms – an idea emphatically rejected by both countries. In 1611 he authorized the translation of the Bible into English, and nine years later the Mayflower pilgrims left for America. James died in 1625.

James VI/I by an unknown artist

Above: *James VI/I attributed to Adrian Vanson*
Right: *James VI/I (detail) by Adam de Colone*

CHARLES I

reigned 1625–1649

Although he grew up in England, Charles (born in 1600) had a Scots tutor and always took a keen interest in the country. Unfortunately, he had little talent for kingship, alienating people on both sides of the border with his insistence that monarchs were appointed by God and had a divine right to rule. When the Civil War broke out in 1641, many Scots fought for the king, but others fought equally bravely for Parliament.

After the Royalist defeat, Charles was offered an honourable peace but tried to start the war again. Exasperated, the Parliamentarians put him on trial for waging war on his own people. He was found guilty by a fixed vote and publicly beheaded in 1649. His execution horrified the Scots, who wished him no personal harm and were outraged that the English had killed a Scottish king without even asking permission.

Charles I by or after Robert Peake
OVERLEAF: *Charles I and James VII/II*
by an unknown artist after Sir Peter Lely

CHARLES II

❖

reigned 1651–1685

England was a republic for eleven years after the execution of Charles I. In Scotland, however, his son Charles II (born in 1630) was crowned with great pomp in 1651. A few months later, Charles led a Scots invasion of England, only to be defeated by Oliver Cromwell and the Parliamentary army at Worcester. He fled to France and never saw Scotland again.

Restored to England in 1660, Charles resolved never to go on his travels again. The Civil War of his childhood left him deeply insecure, determined to make up for lost time by enjoying himself to the full. He had scores of mistresses and fathered numerous illegitimate children. He was much loved by the English as a 'Merry Monarch', but never cared much for Scotland, leaving it to his representatives to run the country on his behalf.

Charles II (detail) by William Dobson

DVKE OF YORK

JAMES VII/II

❖

reigned 1685–1689

Born in 1633, James succeeded his brother at the age of fifty-two. Although he had made two earlier trips to Scotland, he never visited the country as king and was the first monarch in almost 400 years not to be crowned there. He was also a Roman Catholic convert – a recipe for disaster in a fiercely Protestant country, which detested any kind of popery.

At first the Scots gave him their loyal support. But James went too far when he allowed Catholic officers to join the English army and asked the Scottish Parliament to repeal Scotland's anti-Catholic legislation. The English invited James's daughter, Mary, and her Protestant husband, William of Orange, to rule in his place. Scotland's Parliament debated whether to follow suit. From exile in France, James sent the Scots such a tactless ultimatum that they sided with William and Mary. James died in 1701.

James VII/II (detail) by Sir Peter Lely

WILLIAM II/III

※

reigned 1689–1702

Agrandson of Charles I, William of Orange (born in 1650) was a staunch Dutch Protestant married to James VII/II's daughter Mary. She refused to accept the crown unless her husband was joint monarch with her. The Scots agreed, provided the couple ruled constitutionally under the law, and not by divine right.

James invaded Catholic Ireland to try and win back his throne, but was decisively beaten by William at the Boyne in 1690. William never once visited Scotland, preferring to administer the country through his Dutch favourites in London. He was perhaps unfairly blamed for the massacre at Glencoe, when the Campbells murdered the MacDonalds in a breach of Highland hospitality that has never been forgotten. When William died, after his horse slipped on a molehill, Jacobites everywhere raised their glasses to 'the little gentleman in black velvet'.

William II/III attributed to Sir Godfrey Kneller

MARY II

---✣---

reigned 1689–1694

Overshadowed first by her father, then by her dour and humourless husband, Mary (born in 1662) grew up meek and mild, only too happy to leave politics to the men. She wept for days when James told her, aged fifteen, that she was to marry the hunchbacked William. But she later became reconciled to the marriage, although William never treated her as well as he should have done.

Mary greatly resented being forced to accept the throne in place of the father she loved, and in fact never saw again. A devout Protestant, she took no interest in government and knew little of Scotland. Without even any children of her own she depended on her unfaithful husband for everything. Mary's was not a particularly happy life, but she was a decent woman and was genuinely mourned when she died at the age of thirty-two.

Mary II by an unknown artist after Willem Wissing

ANNE

❖

reigned 1702–1714

As the second daughter of James VII/II, Anne (born in 1665) should have succeeded Mary in 1694. Instead, she allowed William to remain on the throne and did not herself become queen until his death in 1702. She was the last officially recognized Stuart monarch and also the last monarch of an independent Scotland.

Anne presided over the Union of England and Scotland in 1707, something both countries had opposed for centuries. The difference now was that the English were at war with the French (who had recognized the legitimacy of James VII/II's son) and therefore threatened the Scots with trade sanctions to force them into a permanent alliance. Anne thought the move would benefit the Scots and was delighted when the crosses of St Andrew and St George were combined in the Union flag. She outlived all of her seventeen children to die in 1714.

Anne (detail) by Willem Wissing and Jan van der Vaardt

JAMES VIII/III

◈

did not reign

Anne was succeeded by Prince George of Hanover, a great-grandson of James VI/I, who spoke no English. Although the Scots recognized him as king, many felt that James VII/II's removal had been unconstitutional and that his son James – the Old Pretender – was therefore the legitimate ruler. These Jacobites toasted 'the King over the water' and longed for his return.

In fact James might have succeeded Anne if he had agreed to renounce Catholicism (his birth in 1688 as a male Catholic heir had precipitated his father's removal from the throne). But James refused, believing that he would one day be legitimately restored, as his uncle Charles II had been. Dull and uncharismatic, he landed in Scotland too late to play any meaningful part in the lacklustre Jacobite rebellion of 1715. He fled back to France and died a broken man in 1766.

James VIII/III by an unknown artist
OVERLEAF: *The Marriage of Prince James Francis Edward Stuart and Princess Clementina Sobieska by Agostino Masucci*

CHARLES III

✥

did not reign

Born in exile in 1720, Bonnie Prince Charlie was good-looking and romantic – a far more appealing figure than his father. He inspired the Jacobite rebellion of 1745, landing in Scotland with just seven companions in a desperate attempt to regain the crown for his family.

The rebellion might have succeeded: a Jacobite army won the battle of Prestonpans and invaded England as far as Derby before deciding to withdraw. It was pursued by professional English troops who crushed the rebellion at Culloden in 1746. Charles spent five months on the run, hidden by Flora MacDonald and other Highlanders, before escaping to France. He turned to the bottle and rapidly lost his good looks. In 1750 he visited London in disguise, secretly converting to Protestantism in an attempt to woo the English. Deserted by everyone except his daughter, he died miserably in 1788.

Charles III by Maurice Quentin de la Tour
OVERLEAF: *Baptism of Prince Charles Edward Stuart*
by Pier Leone Ghezzi

HENRY IX

did not reign

Although he styled himself Henry IX on the death of his brother Charles, Henry Stuart never had any serious illusions about the English and Scottish thrones. Among other things, he was a Roman Catholic priest, something that would hardly have endeared him to his subjects.

Born in 1725, he grew up in Italy, heavily influenced by the religion of his Polish mother. He was a cardinal at the age of twenty-two, and later an archbishop. He never set foot in the British Isles and never caused the government any trouble. Henry lost all his money in the Napoleonic Wars and was destitute until George III of England sent him £2,000. He retired to Frascati, south of Rome, and died a bachelor in 1807. As the last of the male line, he left the Stuart crown jewels in his will to the future George IV.

Henry IX by Antonio David

ELIZABETH I/II

·:·

reigned 1952–

Elizabeth traces her ancestry through
George I to James VI/I and almost all the
Scottish monarchs who went before,
including Duncan. She is descended from
Robert the Bruce through both parents, for her
mother was a Scottish aristocrat, daughter of the Earl
of Strathmore.

Born in 1926, Elizabeth became queen in 1952 and
has always taken a keen interest in Scottish affairs. The
royal family's love affair with Scotland began under
Queen Victoria and shows little sign of abating. The
Queen's three sons all went to school in Scotland, and
so did her eldest grandson. They wear the kilt north of
the border and always spend the summer at Balmoral.

It was during Elizabeth's reign that the Stone of
Scone – a sacred relic stolen from the Scots in 1296 –
was returned to its homeland after 700 years in
Westminster Abbey.

Elizabeth I/II by Sir William Oliphant Hutchison